Kilmanns Team-Gap Survey

RALPH H. KILMANN AND ASSOCIATES

Distributed by
KILMANN DIAGNOSTICS
1 Suprema Drive
Newport Coast, CA 92657
www.kilmanndiagnostics.com
info@kilmanndiagnostics.com
949.497.8766

Introduction

The individuals in any work group have a great deal of knowledge and experience. But the bottom-line question is: Will all this available talent in the group be used to manage business, technical, and organizational problems or will the expertise and information be wasted? This survey allows your work group to identify what might be getting in the way of its daily functioning. Part 1 of the survey asks all members to indicate the *actual* functioning of their group. Part 2 asks all members to indicate the *desired* functioning of their group.

Part 1: Actual Group Functioning

On the following pages, you will see 24 items asking you about the daily functioning of your work group—sorted into four areas: cultural norms, people management, problem management, and time management. For each item, please circle one number—from 1 to 7—that best reflects the **actual** functioning of your group on a daily basis. To help you pinpoint your response to each item, brief descriptions are provided along the seven-point scale.

Note: There are several items that directly concern the boss of the work group. *If you are responding to this survey as a boss* (for example, as a supervisor or a manager), please respond to such items differently: For each item that specifically mentions the boss, try to estimate how the *other* group members will respond on the seven-point scale (on average). Later, you will be able to see how well your estimates compare with the actual perceptions of the other group members.

Actual Cultural Norms

1. To what extent does your group foster a positive, adaptive approach to the need for change and improvement?

1	2	3	4	5	6	7

Most members seem to prefer the "good old days" and frequently complain about all the pressure to change and improve. They have negative attitudes.

While some members seem to be living in the past, others focus on what needs to be done differently for the present and the future.

Most members are moving forward in today's world and encourage others to question their own constant complaining or reluctance to "come on board."

2. To what extent do group members support your efforts to behave according to the desired norms—behavior that fosters the long-term success of the whole organization?

1	2	3	4	5	6	7

They rarely, if ever encourage me to behave according to our desired norms. They largely ignore or avoid the topic.

Sometimes they support my efforts to behave according to our desired norms. But at other times, they ignore or avoid the topic of cultural change.

We have open discussions about desired norms and we help one another to follow our group's cultural guidelines.

3. To what extent do you feel you can give sanctions—positive and negative feedback—to encourage group members to change and improve their behavior on the job?

1	2	3	4	5	6	7

It would be foolish of me to give feedback to my group members. In fact, if I gave them any negative feedback about their reluctance to change, they would give me a lot of grief.

I can give feedback to some of the members of my group. But in many cases, my comments would not be appreciated or well received—especially if I gave any negative feedback.

My group encourages both positive and negative feedback. We help one another to change and improve by pointing out bad habits and celebrating new behavior.

4. What is your group's attitude toward continually learning new ideas and constantly striving to improve its performance?

1	2	3	4	5	6	7

Members are overly content. They feel they are too busy or too effective to worry about learning and improving.

Members recognize that learning is important, but they seem too busy to work at improving quality and performance.

Members place high value on learning and improving. They also take the time and effort to do so on a regular basis.

5. To what extent does your group trust the other groups and departments in the organization—by valuing and respecting their daily work and their overall contributions to the success of the organization?

1	2	3	4	5	6	7

We tend to put down the work of other groups. In some cases, we have serious doubts about their capabilities.

We respect and value some of the groups in the organization. But for the other groups, it is very difficult for us to trust their words or deeds.

We have a lot of respect for all the other groups and departments. We are all part of the same organizational team.

6. To what extent does your group trust management (senior executives and all the other levels of management) to do the right things in the right way for your group and the rest of the organization?

1	2	3	4	5	6	7

We seriously mistrust the motives, intentions, and honesty of our managers. They mostly take care of themselves.

Sometimes they are forthright and do what is in the best interests of the organization. But at other times, they are very political and seem to play the same old games.

We have a lot of trust and faith in our managers. They are working hard to do what is best for us and our organization.

Actual People Management

7. How well does your group manage its differences—including differences in personality style, motivation, approaches to problems, and actual performance?

1	2	3	4	5	6	7

We generally avoid any differences among our group members. We assume that we are all basically the same and should do things similarly.

We recognize some differences in style and approach among group members. But most times we do not openly discuss, or try to understand, differences among us.

We have a deep respect for our differences. We explicitly examine our differences to satisfy members' needs and solve problems.

8. How effective is the boss in keeping the group members up to date on all the things affecting them?

1	2	3	4	5	6	7

Members hear about relevant information from other than the boss or not at all. In some cases, it seems that the boss withholds vital information.

The boss keeps members informed on some issues but not on others. At times, the boss does not provide information that was requested explicitly by group members.

The boss works with members to provide information that they desire on a timely basis. The boss provides whatever vital information is needed to do the job.

9. To what extent do group members acknowledge and respect one another's ego—by being sensitive to the daily struggle that people have with self-esteem and self-worth?

1	2	3	4	5	6	7

We don't give special attention to egos. We don't seem to worry about insecurities and self-doubts. We are tough-minded individuals.	We recognize that anyone can feel insecure on any given day. But we don't change the way we communicate and work with one another.	We are very sensitive to one another's ego. We interact and communicate with one another not only to respect self-esteem but to build it.

10. To what extent does your group treat you like a valued member of the team on a daily basis?

1	2	3	4	5	6	7

I don't feel like an equal member of the team. I seem to be on the outside looking in during most group discussions and meetings.	At times I feel included in the group discussion. But at other times, it seems that my views and opinions are not really respected or appreciated.	I feel like an equal partner in my group. My ideas are valued and team members even go out of their way to get my ideas and opinions.

11. Do you feel comfortable sharing your ideas and opinions with your group members?

1	2	3	4	5	6	7

It would be foolish for me to share my true feelings or viewpoints with group members. I might be ridiculed or criticized in public.	I am cautious about what I share with group members. On some topics I can be open, but on other topics it is best for me to keep silent.	On virtually any topic, I can express my ideas and opinions without any fear of public ridicule or criticism.

12. How well do members communicate with one another during their group meetings and work discussions?

1	2	3	4	5	6	7

Members criticize one another, make one another defensive, and put down any idea that is new or different.	Members show some respect for one another's ego. But new or different ideas tend to receive considerable skepticism.	Members show a definite regard for one another. They also actively support the expression of new and different ideas.

Actual Problem Management

13. To what extent does your group understand its own goals and objectives and how its work fits into the big picture for the whole company?

1	2	3	4	5	6	7

Members have very different views about the purpose of the group. Other than lip-service, very little attention is given to the big picture.

Most members understand the goals and objectives of the group. But there isn't much concern for coordinating our work with other groups or departments.

We periodically clarify our goals and objectives. We also make sure that our work is in sync with the rest of the organization.

14. How effective is your group at involving people from other work groups in the organization when you need additional input, expertise, or resources?

1	2	3	4	5	6	7

We usually overlook the possibility of seeking outside help when we need additional expertise or information on complex problems.

Sometimes we involve people outside our work group on important and complex problems. Often, however, we tend to rely on our own knowledge and experience.

Usually we are quick at identifying and seeking outside help on important and complex problems, rather than relying on our limited view.

15. To what extent does your group first define the root causes of its complex problems *before* it derives solutions and proceeds with action?

1	2	3	4	5	6	7

Faced with virtually any problem, we first discuss different possible solutions and then do our best to implement our chosen solution.

Occasionally, we take a little time to discuss what might be causing the problem. But in most cases, we take our usual approach to fixing what went wrong.

We distinguish simple from complex problems. Then, for the complex ones, we first determine the root causes before we proceed further.

16. To what extent does your group analyze its assumptions when it is faced with recurring problems, unresolved differences, and complex situations?

1	2	3	4	5	6	7

We rarely make our assumptions explicit. Usually, we live with unresolved issues and just keep working at things until they somehow get fixed.

Occasionally we analyze our assumptions. But we only do so when all else fails and we can't live with a bad situation much longer.

On all important, complex, and recurring problems, we explicitly analyze our assumptions so we can get right to the heart of the matter.

17. To what extent does your boss encourage an open, candid, and thorough examination of work group problems?

1	2	3	4	5	6	7

Our boss prefers to avoid problems. Even when we bring problems to the boss's attention, little time or effort is devoted to solving the problem.	Sometimes our boss gets our input on problems and tries to address important issues. But other times, our boss avoids the situation altogether.	Our boss encourages us to bring important problems to his or her attention, so we can address all the key issues both directly and effectively.

18. How much responsibility are members willing to take for their decisions and actions?

1	2	3	4	5	6	7

Group decisions are avoided at all costs. Risks must be at or near zero before members will "own" a decision and take responsibility for its implementation.	Group decisions are made only after considerable discussion. But they may not be implemented as intended. Members are not entirely comfortable with owning the decision or its implementation.	Group decisions are made as required and are implemented as intended. Risks are accepted as a normal price of membership in the work group and the organization.

Actual Time Management

19. How well does your boss clarify—and if necessary change—priorities when work is assigned or when special requests are made?

1	2	3	4	5	6	7

Our boss rarely discusses or clarifies priorities. New work or special requests are simply added on to all other things we are expected to do.

Occasionally, our boss clarifies priorities and makes adjustments. But on a daily basis, work assignments tend to be seriously out of whack with job priorities.

Our boss frequently reviews priorities and quickly makes changes as the work situation requires. Work assignments are in line with priorities.

20. To what extent does your group take the time to plan how it will approach its various projects, tasks, and activities?

1	2	3	4	5	6	7

Virtually no time is devoted to planning our work before we proceed. We simply keep doing what we have been assigned until everything— hopefully—gets done.

We say that planning is important and devote some time to it when we can. But for the most part, we work without sufficient planning.

We don't proceed with action until we plan the best use of our time. Planning is viewed as our most important work: Planning drives what we accomplish.

21. How well does your group manage its meetings?

1	2	3	4	5	6	7

Meetings are loosely planned and mostly unorganized. Discussions jump from topic to topic. Meetings are a waste of time.

Little effort is made to plan our meetings. But after considerable discussion, some decisions are made and some useful results occur.

Meetings are guided by agenda. They start on time, stick to the topic, and end on time. Meetings are productive and satisfying.

22. To what extent does your boss set the proper example for time management on a daily basis—and thereby discourage the use of crisis management?

1	2	3	4	5	6	7

Our boss does not respect his or her own time and priorities. He interrupts our work with special requests or lower-priority work than we have already been assigned.

Occasionally our boss is willing to change priorities when additional work is assigned and is sensitive to our time in other ways. But in many cases, the boss's approach to time management is lacking.

Our boss manages time very well and expects us to do the same. The boss insists that we prioritize and plan our work and does not undermine our efforts at time management.

23. How well does your group draw out the quieter members to make sure that they have the opportunity to contribute to the discussion or decision?

1	2	3	4	5	6	7

The most vocal members tend to dominate our group meetings. If anyone doesn't fight to be heard, he or she will likely be ignored.	Sometimes, the quieter members are asked for their opinions. But most of the time, no one bothers to check if everyone has had a chance to contribute.	In every meeting, one or more members will explicitly ask the quieter members if they would like to add anything to the group discussion.

24. To what extent does your group examine its functioning and make use of an appointed Process Observer to ensure that it continually improves its processes over time?

1	2	3	4	5	6	7

We rarely, if ever, discuss how we are doing as a group and how we could improve. We don't bother to use a Process Observer.	We often use a Process Observer at our group meetings. But we don't take much time to discuss the feedback or how to improve the functioning of our work group.	We use a Process Observer at virtually every group meeting. We also discuss the results and how we can improve our group processes.

Part 2: Desired Group Functioning

On the following pages, you will see the same 24 items asking you about the daily functioning of your work group—sorted into the same four areas: cultural norms, people management, problem management, and time management. For each item, circle one number (from 1 to 7) that best reflects the **desired** functioning of your work group on a daily basis. As before, in order to help you pinpoint your response to each item, brief descriptions are provided along the seven-point scale.

Note: If you are responding to this survey as a boss of the work group (as a supervisor or manager), you should respond to all items in terms of what is desired, including those items that specifically mention the boss. Later, you will be able to find out how well your ideals compare with the desired perceptions of the other group members.

Desired Cultural Norms

25. To what extent does your group foster a positive, adaptive approach to the need for change and improvement?

1	2	3	4	5	6	7

Most members seem to prefer the "good old days" and frequently complain about all the pressure to change and improve. They have negative attitudes.

While some members seem to be living in the past, others focus on what needs to be done differently for the present and the future.

Most members are moving forward in today's world and encourage others to question their own constant complaining or reluctance to "come on board."

26. To what extent do group members support your efforts to behave according to the desired norms—behavior that fosters the long-term success of the whole organization?

1	2	3	4	5	6	7

They rarely, if ever encourage me to behave according to our desired norms. They largely ignore or avoid the topic.

Sometimes they support my efforts to behave according to our desired norms. But at other times, they ignore or avoid the topic of cultural change.

We have open discussions about desired norms and we help one another to follow our group's cultural guidelines.

27. To what extent do you feel you can give sanctions—positive and negative feedback—to encourage group members to change and improve their behavior on the job?

1	2	3	4	5	6	7

It would be foolish of me to give feedback to my group members. In fact, if I gave them any negative feedback about their reluctance to change, they would give me a lot of grief.	I can give feedback to some of the members of my group. But in many cases, my comments would not be appreciated or well received— especially if I gave any negative feedback.	My group encourages both positive and negative feedback. We help one another to change and improve by pointing out bad habits and celebrating new behavior.

28. What is your group's attitude toward continually learning new ideas and constantly striving to improve its performance?

1	2	3	4	5	6	7

Members are overly content. They feel they are too busy or too effective to worry about learning and improving.	Members recognize that learning is important, but they seem too busy to work at improving quality and performance.	Members place high value on learning and improving. They also take the time and effort to do so on a regular basis.

29. To what extent does your group trust the other groups and departments in the organization—by valuing and respecting their daily work and their overall contributions to the success of the organization?

1	2	3	4	5	6	7

We tend to put down the work of other groups. In some cases, we have serious doubts about their capabilities.

We respect and value some of the groups in the organization. But for the other groups, it is very difficult for us to trust their words or deeds.

We have a lot of respect for all the other groups and departments. We are all part of the same organizational team.

30. To what extent does your group trust management (senior executives and all the other levels of management) to do the right things in the right way for your group and the rest of the organization?

1	2	3	4	5	6	7

We seriously mistrust the motives, intentions, and honesty of our managers. They mostly take care of themselves.

Sometimes they are forthright and do what is in the best interests of the organization. But at other times, they are very political and seem to play the same old games.

We have a lot of trust and faith in our managers. They are working hard to do what is best for us and our organization.

Desired People Management

31. How well does your group manage its differences—including differences in personality style, motivation, approaches to problems, and actual performance?

1	2	3	4	5	6	7

We generally avoid any differences among our group members. We assume that we are all basically the same and should do things similarly.

We recognize some differences in style and approach among group members. But most times we do not openly discuss, or try to understand, differences among us.

We have a deep respect for our differences. We explicitly examine our differences to satisfy members' needs and solve problems.

32. How effective is the boss in keeping the group members up to date on all the things affecting them?

1	2	3	4	5	6	7

Members hear about relevant information from other than the boss or not at all. In some cases, it seems that the boss withholds vital information.

The boss keeps members informed on some issues but not on others. At times, the boss does not provide information that was requested explicitly by group members.

The boss works with members to provide information that they desire on a timely basis. The boss provides whatever vital information is needed to do the job.

33. To what extent do group members acknowledge and respect one another's ego—by being sensitive to the daily struggle that people have with self-esteem and self-worth?

1	2	3	4	5	6	7

We don't give special attention to egos. We don't seem to worry about insecurities and self-doubts. We are tough-minded individuals.	We recognize that anyone can feel insecure on any given day. But we don't change the way we communicate and work with one another.	We are very sensitive to one another's ego. We interact and communicate with one another not only to respect self-esteem but to build it.

34. To what extent does your group treat you like a valued member of the team on a daily basis?

1	2	3	4	5	6	7

I don't feel like an equal member of the team. I seem to be on the outside looking in during most group discussions and meetings.	At times I feel included in the group discussion. But at other times, it seems that my views and opinions are not really respected or appreciated.	I feel like an equal partner in my group. My ideas are valued and team members even go out of their way to get my ideas and opinions.

35. Do you feel comfortable sharing your ideas and opinions with your group members?

1	2	3	4	5	6	7

It would be foolish for me to share my true feelings or viewpoints with group members. I might be ridiculed or criticized in public.

I am cautious about what I share with group members. On some topics I can be open, but on other topics it is best for me to keep silent.

On virtually any topic, I can express my ideas and opinions without any fear of public ridicule or criticism.

36. How well do members communicate with one another during their group meetings and work discussions?

1	2	3	4	5	6	7

Members criticize one another, make one another defensive, and put down any idea that is new or different.

Members show some respect for one another's ego. But new or different ideas tend to receive considerable skepticism.

Members show a definite regard for one another. They also actively support the expression of new and different ideas.

Desired Problem Management

37. To what extent does your group understand its own goals and objectives and how its work fits into the big picture for the whole company?

1	2	3	4	5	6	7

Members have very different views about the purpose of the group. Other than lip-service, very little attention is given to the big picture.

Most members understand the goals and objectives of the group. But there isn't much concern for coordinating our work with other groups or departments.

We periodically clarify our goals and objectives. We also make sure that our work is in sync with the rest of the organization.

38. How effective is your group at involving people from other work groups in the organization when you need additional input, expertise, or resources?

1	2	3	4	5	6	7

We usually overlook the possibility of seeking outside help when we need additional expertise or information on complex problems.

Sometimes we involve people outside our work group on important and complex problems. Often, however, we tend to rely on our own knowledge and experience.

Usually we are quick at identifying and seeking outside help on important and complex problems, rather than relying on our limited view.

39. To what extent does your group first define the root causes of its complex problems *before* it derives solutions and proceeds with action?

1	2	3	4	5	6	7

Faced with virtually any problem, we first discuss different possible solutions and then do our best to implement our chosen solution.	Occasionally, we take a little time to discuss what might be causing the problem. But in most cases, we take our usual approach to fixing what went wrong.	We distinguish simple from complex problems. Then, for the complex ones, we first determine the root causes before we proceed further.

40. To what extent does your group analyze its assumptions when it is faced with recurring problems, unresolved differences, and complex situations?

1	2	3	4	5	6	7

We rarely make our assumptions explicit. Usually, we live with unresolved issues and just keep working at things until they somehow get fixed.	Occasionally we analyze our assumptions. But we only do so when all else fails and we can't live with a bad situation much longer.	On all important, complex, and recurring problems, we explicitly analyze our assumptions so we can get right to the heart of the matter.

41. To what extent does your boss encourage an open, candid, and thorough examination of work group problems?

1	2	3	4	5	6	7

Our boss prefers to avoid problems. Even when we bring problems to the boss's attention, little time or effort is devoted to solving the problem.	Sometimes our boss gets our input on problems and tries to address important issues. But other times, our boss avoids the situation altogether.	Our boss encourages us to bring important problems to his or her attention, so we can address all the key issues both directly and effectively.

42. How much responsibility are members willing to take for their decisions and actions?

1	2	3	4	5	6	7

Group decisions are avoided at all costs. Risks must be at or near zero before members will "own" a decision and take responsibility for its implementation.	Group decisions are made only after considerable discussion. But they may not be implemented as intended. Members are not entirely comfortable with owning the decision or its implementation.	Group decisions are made as required and are implemented as intended. Risks are accepted as a normal price of membership in the work group and the organization.

Desired Time Management

43. How well does your boss clarify—and if necessary change—priorities when work is assigned or when special requests are made?

1	2	3	4	5	6	7

Our boss rarely discusses or clarifies priorities. New work or special requests are simply added on to all other things we are expected to do.

Occasionally, our boss clarifies priorities and makes adjustments. But on a daily basis, work assignments tend to be seriously out of whack with job priorities.

Our boss frequently reviews priorities and quickly makes changes as the work situation requires. Work assignments are in line with priorities.

44. To what extent does your group take the time to plan how it will approach its various projects, tasks, and activities?

1	2	3	4	5	6	7

Virtually no time is devoted to planning our work before we proceed. We simply keep doing what we have been assigned until everything— hopefully—gets done.

We say that planning is important and devote some time to it when we can. But for the most part, we work without sufficient planning.

We don't proceed with action until we plan the best use of our time. Planning is viewed as our most important work: Planning drives what we accomplish.

45. How well does your group manage its meetings?

1	2	3	4	5	6	7

Meetings are loosely planned and mostly unorganized. Discussions jump from topic to topic. Meetings are a waste of time.	Little effort is made to plan our meetings. But after considerable discussion, some decisions are made and some useful results occur.	Meetings are guided by agenda. They start on time, stick to the topic, and end on time. Meetings are productive and satisfying.

46. To what extent does your boss set the proper example for time management on a daily basis—and thereby discourage the use of crisis management?

1	2	3	4	5	6	7

Our boss does not respect his or her own time and priorities. He interrupts our work with special requests or lower-priority work than we have already been assigned.	Occasionally our boss is willing to change priorities when additional work is assigned and is sensitive to our time in other ways. But in many cases, the boss's approach to time management is lacking.	Our boss manages time very well and expects us to do the same. The boss insists that we prioritize and plan our work and does not undermine our efforts at time management.

47. How well does your group draw out the quieter members to make sure that they have the opportunity to contribute to the discussion or decision?

1	2	3	4	5	6	7

The most vocal members tend to dominate our group meetings. If anyone doesn't fight to be heard, he or she will likely be ignored.	Sometimes, the quieter members are asked for their opinions. But most of the time, no one bothers to check if everyone has had a chance to contribute.	In every meeting, one or more members will explicitly ask the quieter members if they would like to add anything to the group discussion.

48. To what extent does your group examine its functioning and make use of an appointed Process Observer to ensure that it continually improves its processes over time?

1	2	3	4	5	6	7

We rarely, if ever, discuss how we are doing as a group and how we could improve. We don't bother to use a Process Observer.	We often use a Process Observer at our group meetings. But we don't take much time to discuss the feedback or how to improve the functioning of our work group.	We use a Process Observer at virtually every group meeting. We also discuss the results and how we can improve our group processes.

Scoring Your Responses

On the following page is your scoring sheet. Just transfer the numbers you circled on the previous pages of this survey. You will find it easiest to transfer Part 1 first (item 1 to 24) and then Part 2 next (item 25 to 48). Naturally, it is essential that you accurately transfer every number.

For each pair of numbers in the columns labeled *Team-Gap*, calculate the absolute difference—by subtracting the two numbers while disregarding the sign. (The absolute difference between 5 and 7 = 2, not −2.) Then add each of the four *Team-Gap* columns. The resulting four sums are your scores for Cultural Norms, People Management, Problem Management, and Time Management. The significance of these four team-gaps will be discussed shortly.

TEAM-GAP SURVEY

PART 2	PART 1	*Team-Gap*		PART 2	PART 1	*Team-Gap*
25 ___	1 ___	*25/1* ___		31 ___	7 ___	*31/7* ___
26 ___	2 ___	*26/2* ___		32 ___	8 ___	*32/8* ___
27 ___	3 ___	*27/3* ___		33 ___	9 ___	*33/9* ___
28 ___	4 ___	*28/4* ___		34 ___	10 ___	*34/10* ___
29 ___	5 ___	*29/5* ___		35 ___	11 ___	*35/11* ___
30 ___	6 ___	*30/6* ___		36 ___	12 ___	*36/12* ___

Cultural Norms

People Management

PART 2	PART 1	*Team-Gap*		PART 2	PART 1	*Team-Gap*
37 ___	13 ___	*37/13* ___		43 ___	19 ___	*43/19* ___
38 ___	14 ___	*38/14* ___		44 ___	20 ___	*44/20* ___
39 ___	15 ___	*39/15* ___		45 ___	21 ___	*45/21* ___
40 ___	16 ___	*40/16* ___		46 ___	22 ___	*46/22* ___
41 ___	17 ___	*41/17* ___		47 ___	23 ___	*47/23* ___
42 ___	18 ___	*42/18* ___		48 ___	24 ___	*48/24* ___

Problem Management

Time Management

Graphing Your Scores

On the following page, please record each of your four scores in the corner space provided by its corresponding team-gap. Naturally, it is essential that you accurately transfer each score.

Plot each of your four scores along the diagonal scale associated with each team-gap. If your score for Cultural Norms is 20, for example, you would circle the hash mark on the top-left diagonal line representing this number. If your score for People Management is 15, you would circle the hash mark on the top-right diagonal representing this number, and so on for Problem Management and Time Management.

Once you have plotted all four of your scores on the graph, connect all four points. This figure shows both the absolute and relative size of all four team-gaps.

TEAM-GAP SURVEY

My Team-Gap Profile

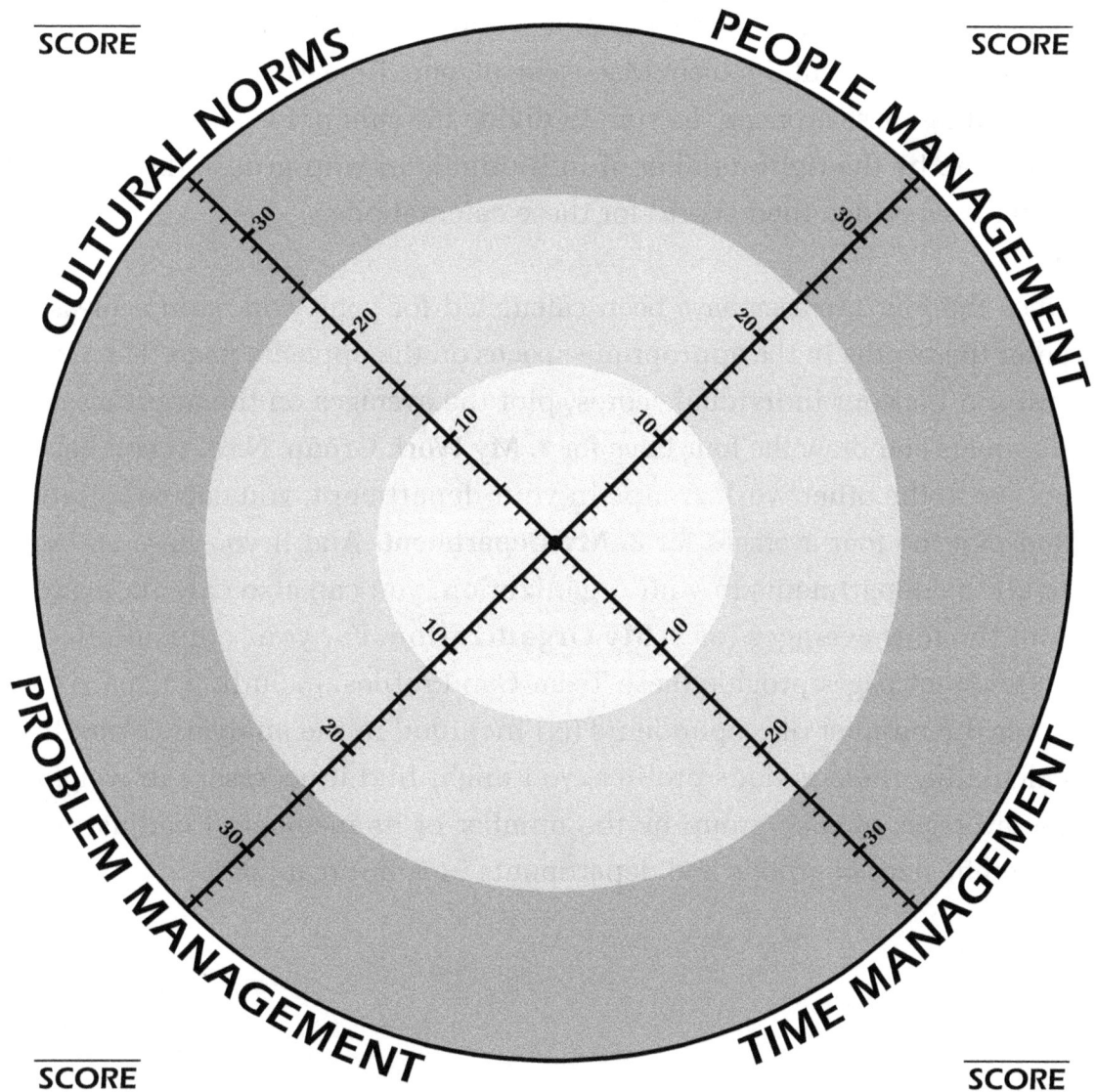

CULTURAL NORMS

PEOPLE MANAGEMENT

30
20
10

30
20
10

10
20
30

10
20
30

PROBLEM MANAGEMENT

TIME MANAGEMENT

Developing Organizational Profiles

Once all the individuals in your work group have obtained and graphed their four team-gaps, collect their numbers together on a separate sheet of paper and calculate four averages: a group average for Cultural Norms, People Management, Problem Management, and Time Management. While computing these averages, be sure to divide the sum of the scores for each team-gap by the right number of individuals in your group: those who actually provided their scores for these calculations.

Once the four averages have been calculated for your work group, please enter the results in the appropriate spaces on the opposite page. Then, as you did for your individual scores, plot the averages on the appropriate diagonals and draw the four lines for **1. My Work Group**. Next, if you have access to the other work groups in your department, you can calculate and plot the four averages for **2. My Department**. And if you have access to all the departments in your organization, you can also calculate and plot the four averages for **3. My Organization**. For your convenience, subsequent pages provide these Team-Gap Profiles, including a space to enter the number of respondents (N) included in the analysis. *Note:* In calculating these various profiles, you might find it necessary to weight the averages of each group by the number of its members to adjust for different sizes of groups and departments in your organization.

TEAM-GAP SURVEY

1. My Work Group (N = _____)

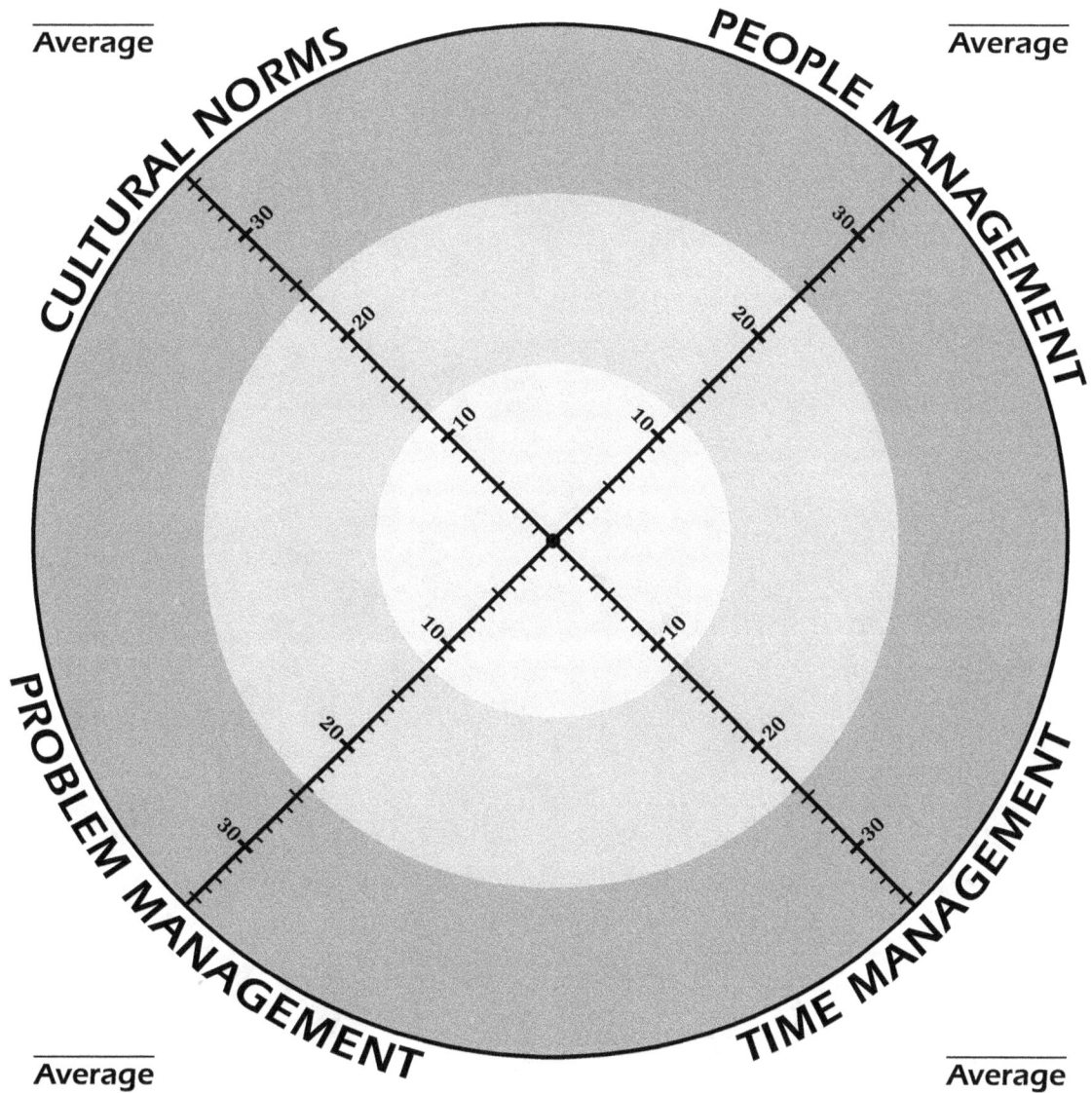

2. My Department (N = _____)

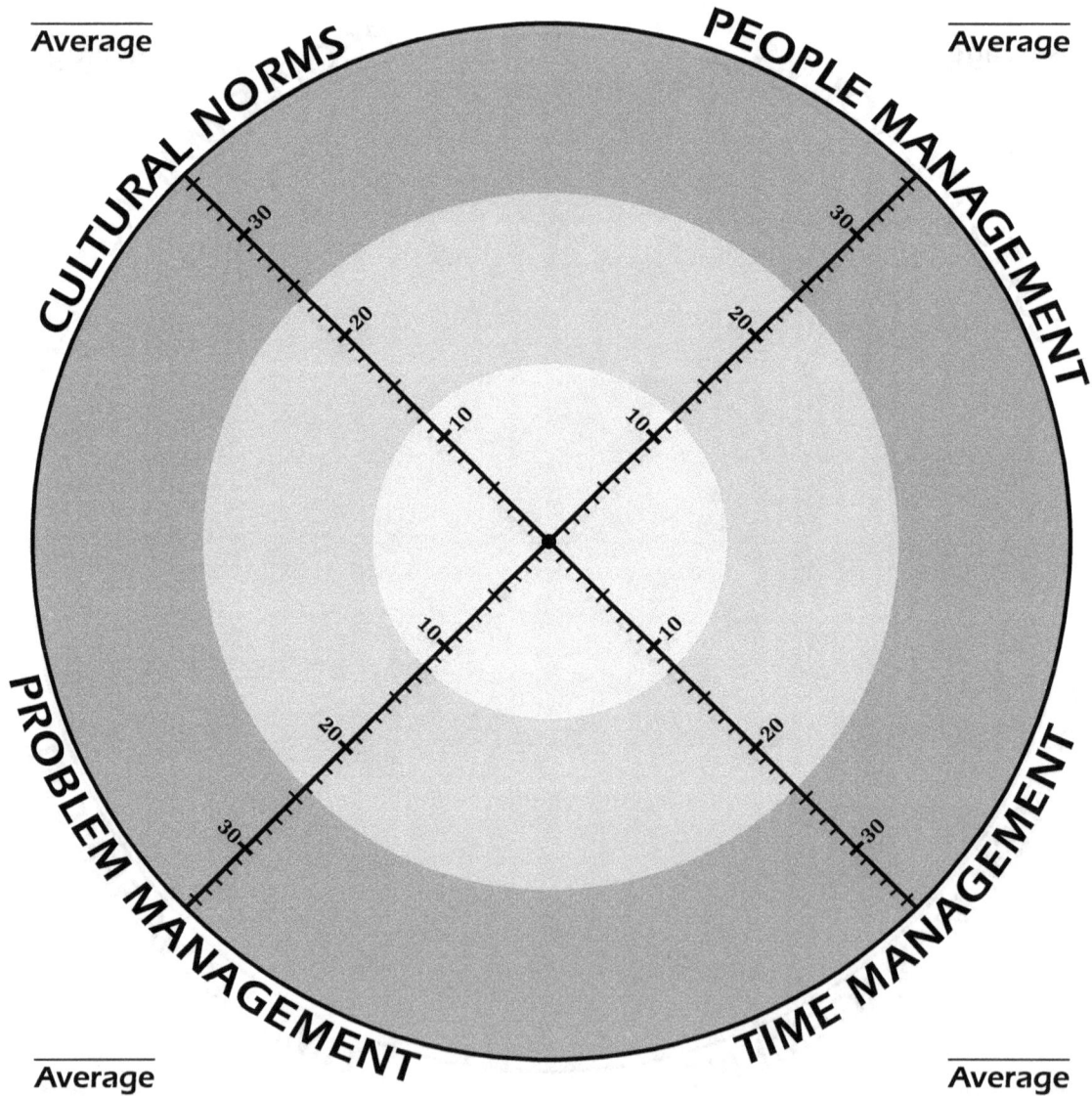

Average

CULTURAL NORMS

PEOPLE MANAGEMENT

Average

30

30

20

20

10

10

10

10

20

20

30

30

PROBLEM MANAGEMENT

TIME MANAGEMENT

Average

Average

3. My Organization (N = _____)

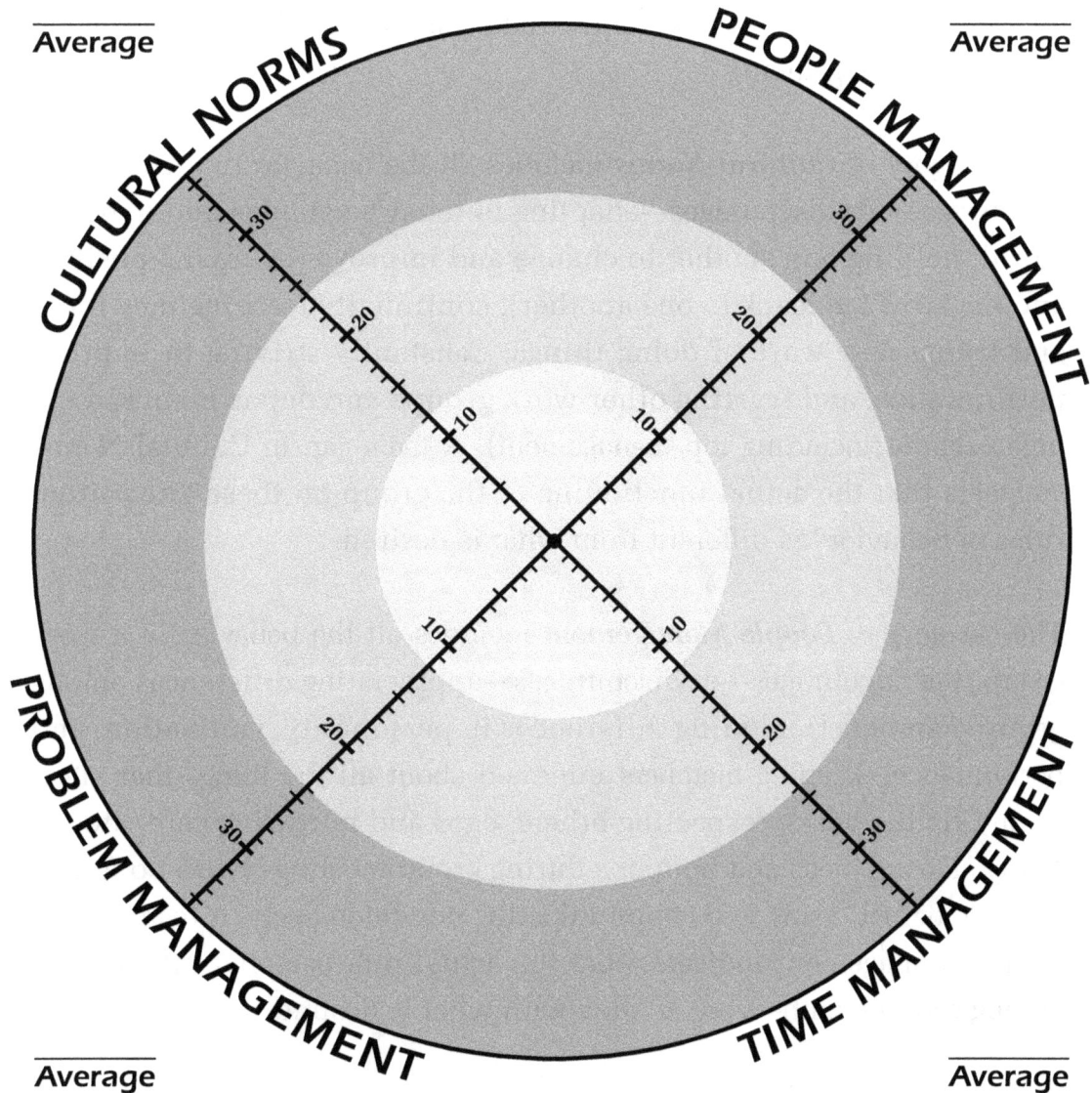

CULTURAL NORMS

PEOPLE MANAGEMENT

30

30

20

20

10

10

10

10

20

20

30

30

PROBLEM MANAGEMENT

TIME MANAGEMENT

Defining Four Team-Gaps

The on-the-job behavior that helps a group accomplish its mission—or, alternatively, what gets in the way—can be organized into four major categories: Cultural Norms, People Management, Problem Management, and Time Management.

The category of *Cultural Norms* includes all the behavior in a group that encourages—or discourages—adapting to today's complex and dynamic world, helping one another to change and improve (by giving positive and negative feedback to one another), continually learning new ideas and trying new ways of doing things, constantly striving to improve performance, and trusting other work groups and departments in the organization (including top management). A team-gap in Cultural Norms suggests that the actual functioning of the group on these "unwritten rules of behavior" is different from what is desired.

The category of *People Management* includes all the behavior in a work group that encourages—or discourages—appreciating differences among group members (including differences in personality, motivation, and performance), keeping members informed about all the things that affect them (via the boss), respecting others' egos and nurturing self-esteem, freely sharing ideas and opinions during group meetings (with no fear of ridicule or criticism), and communicating nondefensively. A team-gap in People Management indicates that the actual interpersonal interactions among group members are at odds with what is desired.

The category of **Problem Management** includes all the behavior that encourages—or discourages—clarifying the group's goals and objectives, involving other people and work groups that have relevant information and expertise to solve problems, defining problems before taking action, analyzing assumptions when problems are complex (or are recurring), examining problems in an open and thorough manner (via the boss), and taking responsibility for decisions and actions. A team-gap in Problem Management indicates that the group's actual approach to addressing its problems is different from what is desired.

The category of **Time Management** includes all the behavior in the work group that encourages—or discourages—clarifying and adjusting job priorities, planning how projects and activities will be coordinated, planning and organizing work group meetings and group discussions, setting the proper example for time management (via the boss), gaining the contribution of the quieter members in the group, and analyzing and improving group processes. A team-gap in Time Management suggests that the group's actual use of its time is different from its desired use.

Interpreting Your Scores

Each team-gap score can vary from 0 to 36, since there are six items per team-gap and the difference between actual group functioning (Part 1) and desired group functioning (Part 2) can vary from 0 (no difference) to 6 (the maximum difference between 1 and 7 on the response scale).

A score (or average) less than 12 represents an insignificant team-gap: The difference between actual and desired group functioning is small (shown by the **mild shading** on the graph). A score (or average) between 12 and 24, however, represents a significant team-gap: The difference between actual and desired group functioning is medium (shown by the **moderate shading** on the graph). A score (or average) greater than 24 represents a highly significant team-gap: The difference between actual and desired group functioning is large (shown by the **dark shading**).

One significant team-gap can interfere with the effective functioning of any work group—for example, mistrusting other groups and departments, not treating group members with respect, not defining problems before taking action, or not planning and organizing group meetings will divert the time and attention of group members. Several significant team-gaps will divert the talent and experience of group members in a number of ways. And worse yet, if all four team-gaps are significant (or highly significant), it will be virtually impossible for the work group to achieve its mission—and thereby contribute to the organization.

On the opposite page is an example of a work group that experiences insignificant team-gaps in all four categories:

TEAM-GAP SURVEY

An Example: My Work Group (N = 8)

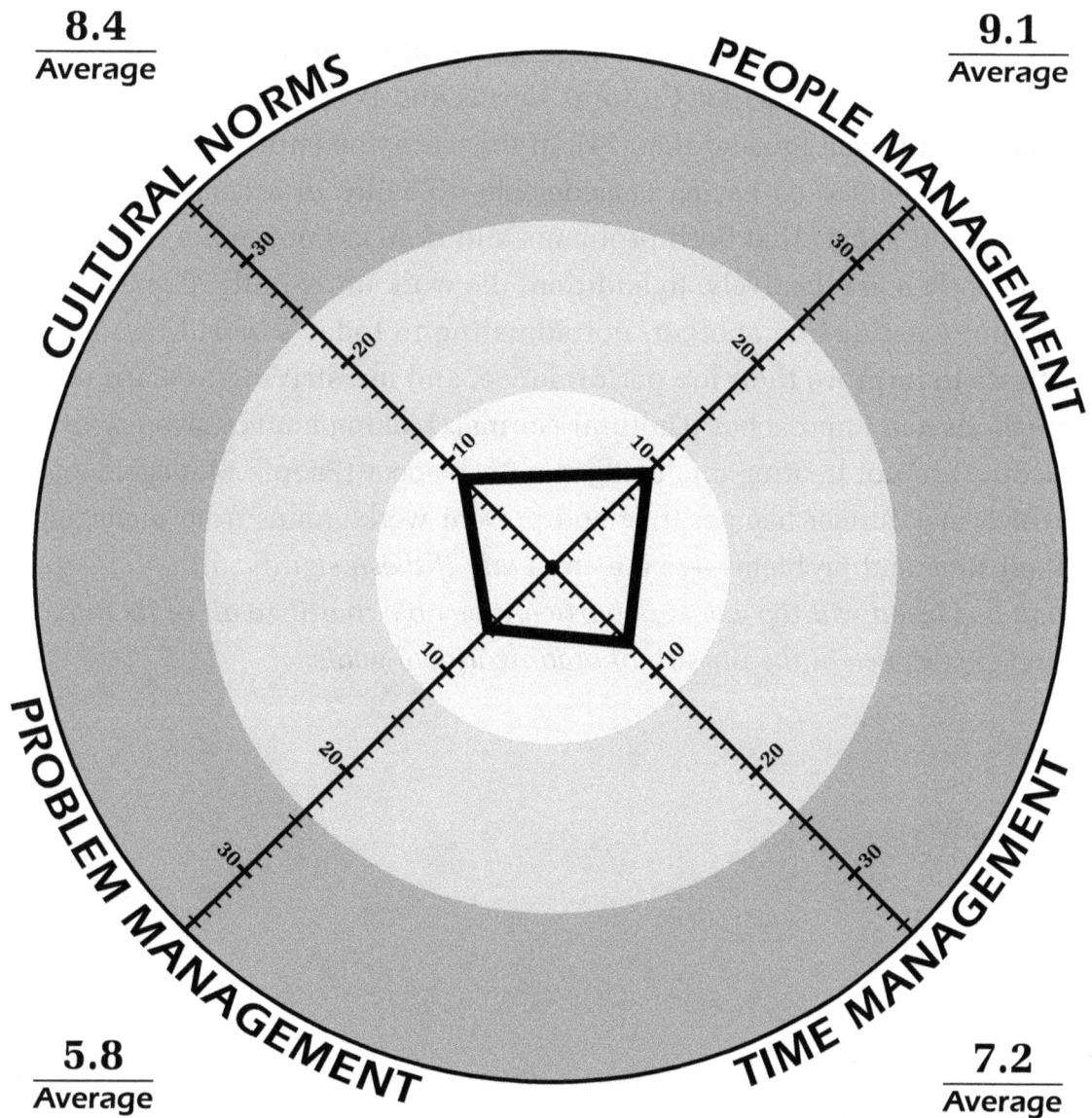

$\dfrac{8.4}{\text{Average}}$

$\dfrac{9.1}{\text{Average}}$

$\dfrac{5.8}{\text{Average}}$

$\dfrac{7.2}{\text{Average}}$

CULTURAL NORMS

PEOPLE MANAGEMENT

PROBLEM MANAGEMENT

TIME MANAGEMENT

30 20 10 10 20 30

Interpreting Your Scores (Continued)

On the opposite page is an example of a department that has significant team-gaps in all four categories: Although the team-gaps for Problem Management and Time Management are clearly significant (between 12 and 24), the team-gaps for Cultural Norms and People Management are *highly* significant (greater than 24). In this case, the entire department— on average—must be having considerable difficulty in accomplishing its mission. It seems that both problems and time are not being managed efficiently and effectively. In addition, the work units in the department are not trusting one another, not adjusting to today's world, ignoring efforts to improve their job performance, and not striving to learn new methods and approaches (Cultural Norms). Making matters even worse, people are not treating one another with respect (People Management), which may further hamper trust and prevent work groups from managing their time and problems—as a team. *Only if these significant team-gaps can be closed will the whole department be able to utilize all of its talent and experience in the pursuit of organizational goals.*

TEAM-GAP SURVEY

Another Example: My Department (N = 58)

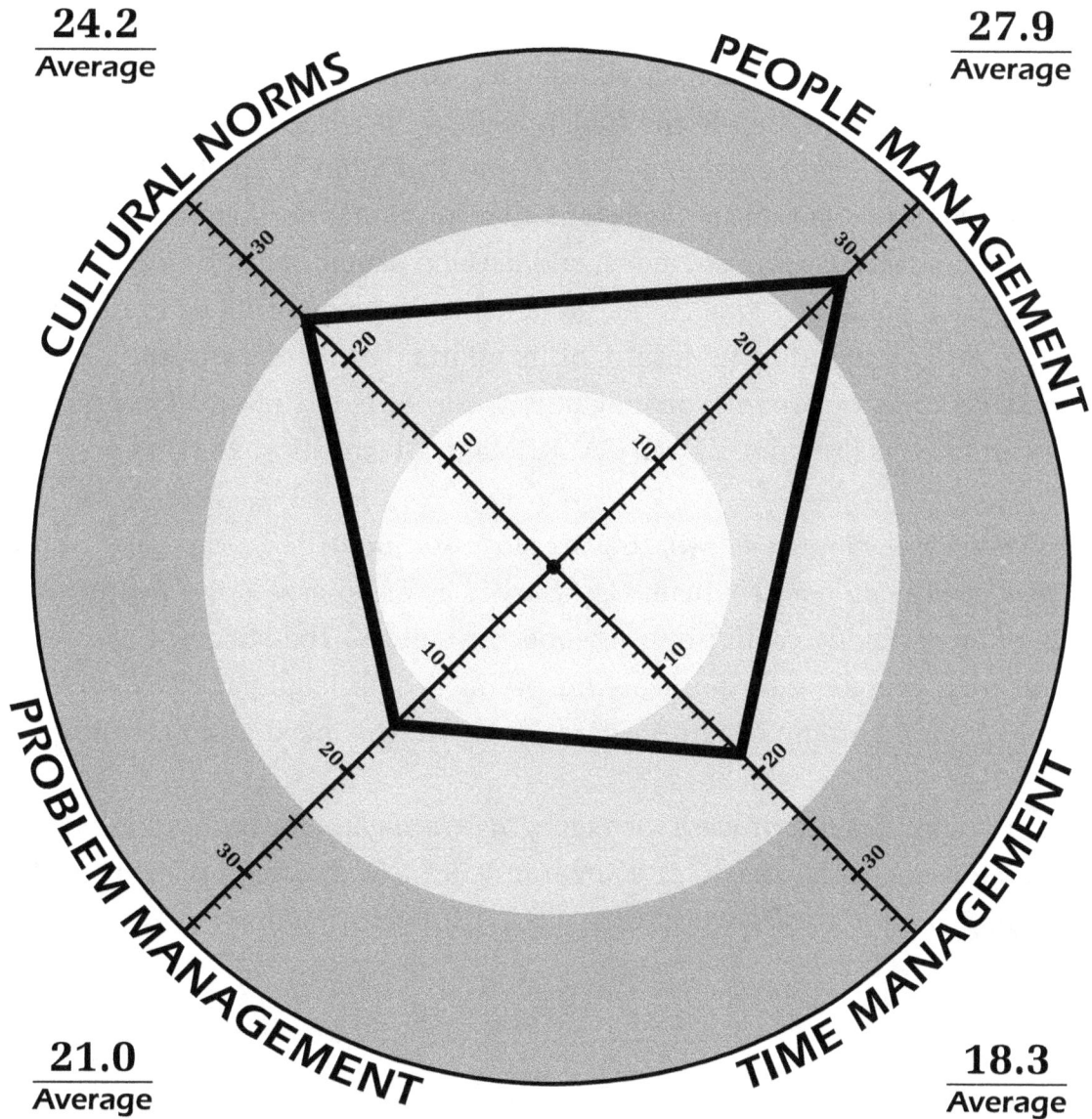

24.2 / Average — CULTURAL NORMS

27.9 / Average — PEOPLE MANAGEMENT

21.0 / Average — PROBLEM MANAGEMENT

18.3 / Average — TIME MANAGEMENT

Closing Team-Gaps

Once a work group (or department) has surveyed its team-gaps, taking special note of any team-gaps that are significant (or highly significant), it's in the best position to close gaps. First the group should discuss what impact its significant team-gaps are having on its daily functioning. Next the group should examine the root causes of these team-gaps: How did these barriers to success come into being and what keeps them alive? Then the group should derive alternative solutions for closing its team-gaps, select one or more solutions, and develop action plans to implement the chosen solutions. Finally, the group must implement its action plans and carefully monitor the results of its efforts. For further discussion of the five steps of problem management, see R. H. Kilmann: *Quantum Organizations* (Newport Coast, CA: Kilmann Diagnostics, 2011).

After several months of working to close its identified team-gaps, the work group can use the Team-Gap Survey again to assess the results of its efforts. Having each group member respond to the survey a second time will provide a sound basis for noting which team-gaps have been closed (have become insignificant) and which ones need more attention.

To use a systematic process for managing team-gaps for both a first and second assessment, see: R. H. Kilmann: *Work Sheets for Identifying and Closing Team-Gaps* (Newport Coast, CA: Kilmann Diagnostics, 2011).

Assessment Tools for the Eight Tracks
Distributed by Kilmann Diagnostics

Kilmann-Saxton Culture-Gap® Survey

Kilmanns Organizational Belief Survey

Kilmanns Time-Gap Survey

Kilmanns Team-Gap Survey

Organizational Courage Assessment

Kilmann-Covin Organizational Influence Survey

Plus the Online Version of the

Thomas-Kilmann Conflict Mode Instrument

Plus These Training and Development Tools

Work Sheets for Identifying and Closing Culture-Gaps

Work Sheets for Identifying and Closing Team-Gaps

And the Book That Fully Explains the Eight Tracks

Quantum Organizations